Copyright © 2021 Daniel Watson.

All rights reserved. No part of this publication may be reproduced, distributed, or transmitted in any form or by any means, including photocopying, recording, or other electronic or mechanical methods, without the prior written permission of the publisher, except in the case of brief quotations embodied in critical reviews and certain other noncommercial uses permitted by copyright law. For permission requests, write to the publisher, addressed "Attention: Permissions Coordinator," at the address below.

ISBN: 978-0-578-98742-2 (Paperback)

Any references to historical events, real people, or real places are used fictitiously. Names, characters, and places are products of the author's imagination.

Front cover image by Riley & Co. Coaching and Design.
Book design by Riley & Co. Coaching and Design.

Printed by okWord Publishing, in the United States of America.

First printing edition 2021.

Daniel Bryant Watson
P O Box 40404
New Bedford, MA 02744

www.dbryantwatson.com

The River

The Sun stopped by my window for our regular morning chat. Peeking through the curtains, he tickled my face to wake me up.

With a laugh and a yawn, which is so odd to do at the same time, I sat up and received his morning wisdom.

"My light only lasts for a short while before I must move on to share it with others. As I spread my joy today, where will you leave yours?"

Hmm, I thought. Not sure of my answer, I thanked the Sun and went to brush my teeth. As I scrubbed to the tune of the ABCs, it hit me. I know exactly what I should do today.

Excited at the promise of an adventure, I rushed to get dressed, and even more quickly dashed out of the door to the path that led from my house to the forest.

But then I noticed a shadow.
Puzzled I thought,
"Shouldn't it be behind me?"

I looked up and laughed at my good friend, Cloud. He asked, "Where are you off to, in such a hurry?"

I answered, "Sun challenged me this morning and it gave me an idea."

Cloud snickered, "That Sun is always up to something. Also, it's getting warm. If you need some shade later, give me a shout."
"Thank you Cloud," I replied.

With the race renewed, soon I was at the entrance to the forest and without a second thought, I plunged in and dove headfirst into the dirt. "So that's what dirt tastes like," I thought to myself.

Unruffled and not even the slightest bit bothered, I dusted myself off and continued on the winding route to my destination.

In a few minutes time, the trees parted
and revealed a treasure.
Making more noise than the birds singing,
insects shuffling and
the animals foraging through the brush,
the River roared her part in the symphony of the woods.

The River was in the midst of her gymnastics routine, flipping and cartwheeling over the stones in her stream, even occasionally backflipping off the edge of her soiled boundaries. The sound of her waves was glorious and I saw that the Sun had come as well, to dance to her melody.

I looked up and asked,
"Sun, how did you know I was coming here?"

Sun giggled and replied,
"A little bird told me."

"Really Sun?"
I shook my head and laughed along.

"So what do you plan to do?" Sun asked.

I sat on the edge of the River, rolled up my jeans and dropped my soil-dusted feet into her flow and answered Sun.

"You asked me where I would leave my joy. My joy is something I can't just leave anywhere. I have to carry it with me always."

"She sang and I listened. I was mesmerized by her rhythm, buffeted by every note, and comforted by her words. They burrowed into my heart, found a comfy spot, and refused to leave. Today, I will share with her the joy she unknowingly bestowed upon me."

"May I join you?"
the Sun asked.

"Do you know the song?"
I replied.

"I'll figure it out,"
he replied knowingly.

And with that, we sang at the top of our lungs!!!

My joy poured out and mingled with the Sun's.

It must have been something because Cloud hovered at the edge of the trees, for only a moment, before he jumped in.

A four-part harmony.

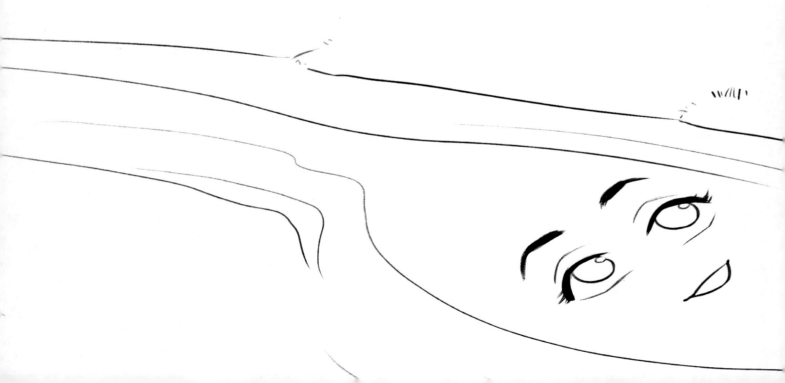

As we got lost in the song, I noticed that one part got softer and softer. I noticed that River had slowed until she became still.

I stopped singing.

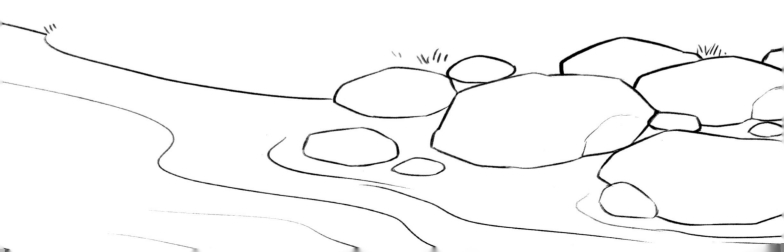

River said quietly, "Please. Keep singing. I have waited a long time for someone to learn my song. All this time, I have only heard myself sing it, so I never knew if it was any good."

A moment's time passed and I stood up and said to River, "Sun, Cloud, and I have heard your song and now it is ours. Everyone who we meet will hear it and will know your joy. This joy that is now ours.
It is good."

the end.

Dedicated to Mommy, my River.

About the Author

DBW is a writer from Boston, MA who experiences life through a magnifying glass at high noon. With a burning desire to take his readers through the convex corners of his imagination, his goal is to illustrate the common human experience from an awkward angle. May you see as never before.

Made in the USA
Middletown, DE
11 November 2021